I Am

Des Taylor

Copyright © 2017 by Des Taylor

All rights reserved

Rejoice Essential Publishing
P.O. BOX 85
Bennettsville, SC 29512
www.republishing.org

All rights reserved. No part of this book may be used or reproduced by any means, graphic, electronic, or mechanical, including photocopying, recording, taping or by any information storage retrieval system without the written permission of the publisher except in the case of brief quotations embodied in critical articles and reviews.

Scriptures taken from the Holy Bible, New International Version®, NIV®. Copyright © 1973, 1978, 1984, 2011 by Biblica, Inc.™ Used by permission of Zondervan. All rights reserved worldwide. www.zondervan.com™

"Scripture quotations taken from the Amplified® Bible (AMP), Copyright © 2015 by The Lockman Foundation Used by permission. www.Lockman.org"

Scripture taken from the New King James Version®. Copyright © 1982 by Thomas Nelson. Used by permission. All rights reserved.

Scripture quotations marked "KJ21" are taken from the 21st Century King James Version®, copyright © 1994. Used by permission of Deuel Enterprises, Inc., Gary, SD 57237. All rights reserved.

Scripture quotations taken from the New American Standard Bible® (NASB), Copyright © 1960, 1962, 1963, 1968, 1971, 1972, 1973, 1975, 1977, 1995 by The Lockman Foundation www.Lockman.org"

Used by permission.

Scripture quotations taken from the New American Standard Bible® (NASB), Copyright © 1960, 1962, 1963, 1968, 1971, 1972, 1973, 1975, 1977, 1995 by The Lockman Foundation .Used by permission. www.Lockman.org

Scripture quotations marked "KJV" are taken from the Holy Bible, King James Version (Public Domain)

Scripture quotations marked "KJ2000" are taken from King James 2000 Bible. The King James 2000 Bible, copyright © Doctor of Theology Robert A. Couric 2000, 2003 Used by permision. All rights reserved.

Scripture quotations marked "NLT" are taken from Holy Bible, New Living Translation, copyright © 1996, 2004, 2007, 2013, 2015 by Tyndale House Foundation. Used by permission of Tyndale House Publishers Inc., Carol Stream, Illinois 60188. All rights reserved.

I Am/ Des Taylor
ISBN-10: 1-946756-14-8
ISBN-13: 978-1-946756-14-5

Library of Congress Control Number: 2017958488

Acknowledgements

To my parents who taught me; to my siblings who encourage me; to the teachers, pastors, and divine connections who inspire me; and to father God, who has shown me who I AM.

Contents

Preface 1

Illustration 4

Confident 5

Witty 6

Intelligent 7

Hard Working 8

Kind & Encouraging 9

Creative & Talented 10

Ambitious 12

Sexy & Stylish 13

Illustration 15

Fearless 16

A Survivor 17

Patient 18

Unstoppable 19

Amazing 20

Brillant	21
Funny	22
A Great Mother	23
A Great Daughter	24
A Great Friend	25
Illustration	26
A Great Advice Giver	27
Motivated & Energetic	28
Inspirational	30
Independent	31
A Genius	32
Determined	33
Wise, Smart, & Forward Thinking	35
Educated & Innovative	37
Illustration	39
A Great Home Maker	40
Goal Orientated & A High Achiever	41
Beautiful	42
A Heroine	44

Stable...45

Entertaining..46

Strong, Courageous, & Bold............................47

An Overcomer..49

Adventurous...51

A Leader...53

Illustration...55

Healed...56

Powerful..58

Happy & Healthy..60

Prosperous & Wealthy....................................62

Resilient..64

A Masterpiece & One-of-a-Kind......................66

Worthy Of Love, Honor, & Respect.................68

Illustration..70

Plan Of Salvation..71

Des Taylor

Preface

In the book of Exodus [chapter 3], Moses in his later years is confronted by God through a burning bush on the mountain of Horeb. The familiar passage lets us know that God called Moses as the chosen vessel to lead the Israelites out of slavery from Egypt. God wanted Moses to tell Pharaoh: "Let my people go."

Like many of us, Moses had his insecurities; he even made excuses as to why he should not be "the one" to fulfill God's unique plan. Moses essentially asked God, "What shall I say to the people, if they ask me who you are [Exodus

3:13]?" God told Moses to say, "I AM THAT I AM. I AM hath sent me unto you [Exodus 3:14]." God's words spoke of authority and confidence in HIS identity. In other words, God knew who he was, and wanted Moses to realize the same!

This book can be used as a tool to help you to regain the confidence that you may have lost through various circumstances such as: bad relationships, brokenness, abuse, low self-esteem, setbacks, sickness and general life issues. We've all experienced sadness, disappointments, struggles, and detours; however, with God's help, we are more than conquerors and have hope! Speak the phrases on each page as much as needed – saying them in the mirror, until the words have penetrated deeply into your soul!

Just as God told Moses, "I AM," believe today that you are what you say and believe in your heart to be [Proverbs 23:7; 4:24; Job 22:28; Luke 6:45]. No matter what you're facing, choose today to live a life of abundance, joy, confidence, and total victory [Prov. 8:21]! It's all in what you speak!

ONE
Confident

"For the Lord will be your confidence, firm and strong, and will keep your foot from being caught [in a trap]." – Prov. 3:26 (AMP)

"Be strong and confident and courageous ..." – Joshua 1:6 (AMP)

• Confidence in yourself and your abilities is not arrogance! Believe in yourself and believe you can achieve God's best – through His help!

TWO

Witty

"I praise you because I am fearfully and wonderfully made; your works are wonderful, I know that full well." — *Psalm 139:14 (NIV)*

- Girl, you're funny, charming and know how to work it! When you enter the room, heads turn! There is truly no one like you!

THREE

Intelligent

"But I have intelligence as well as you; I am not inferior to you. And [a]who does not know such things as these?" – Job 12:3 (NASB)

"He changes times and seasons; he disposes kings and raises up others. He gives wisdom to the wise and knowledge to the understanding." – Daniel 2:21 (NIV)

- You are intelligent! You are brilliant! You can do anything you set your mind to!

FOUR
Hard Working

"Go to the ant, you sluggard; consider its ways and be wise! It has no commander, no overseer or ruler, yet it stores its provisions in summer and gathers its food at harvest." —Proverbs 6:6-8 (NIV)

- With determination, focus and hard work, you can achieve your dreams! You are your only competition!

FIVE
Kind & Encouraging

"May the Lord repay you for your kindness, and may your reward be full from the Lord, the God of Israel, under whose wings you have come to take refuge."— Ruth 2:12 (AMP)

"A generous person will prosper; whoever refreshes others will be refreshed."— Proverbs 11:25 (NIV)

- Don't you know that your words bring life or death to your situation? Speak and think positively, and positive will be the result!

SIX
Creative & Talented

"Then the Lord answered me and said, Write the vision And engrave it plainly on [clay] tablets So that the one who reads it will run."— Habakkuk 2:2 (AMP)

"Where there is no vision [no revelation of God and His word], the people are unrestrained; But happy and blessed is he who keeps the law [of God]."— Proverbs 29:18 (AMP)

• You are truly gifted and have so much to share with the world! Embrace your gifts, hone your skills, and get out there and make your mark!

SEVEN
Ambitious

"I press on toward the goal to win the [heavenly] prize of the upward call of God in Christ Jesus."— Philippians 3:14 (AMP)

- It's okay to be ambitious! It's okay to have big dreams and go after them! No one else can do what you do, SO DO IT!

EIGHT
Sexy & Stylish

"I also clothed you with embroidered cloth and put sandals of [a]porpoise skin on your feet; and I wrapped you with fine linen and covered you with silk. I adorned you with ornaments and I put bracelets on your wrists and a necklace around your neck. I also put a ring in your nostril and earrings in your ears and a beautiful crown on your head. Thus you were adorned with gold and silver, and your dress was [made] of fine linen and silk and embroidered cloth. You ate fine flour and honey and oil; so you were extremely beautiful and you advanced and prospered into royalty."— Ezekiel 16:10-13 (AMP)

- Wow, you are gorgeous! Every feature and every hair was put in place by God – on purpose! Don't you dare compare yourself to anyone else! Be and do you! Buy a new outfit or get a new hairstyle, to let your beauty shine through!

I Am

NINE
Fearless

"For God has not given us a spirit of fear, but of power and of love and of a sound mind."—2 Timothy 1:7 (NKJV)

- Franklin D. Roosevelt once stated, "There is nothing to fear but fear itself!"[1] Don't be afraid to step out, because God is with you!

TEN

A Survivor

"We are troubled on every side, yet not distressed; we are perplexed, but not in despair; persecuted, but not forsaken; cast down, but not destroyed;"
—2 Corinthians 4:8-9 (KJ21)

- Everything you've gone through has made you stronger, wiser, and better! You've gone through what you've gone through (and survived) to help someone else!

ELEVEN
Patient

"Let patience have its perfect work, that you may be perfect and complete, lacking nothing." — James 1:4 (NKJV)

- In this life, it takes patience to achieve your goals, but you can do it! Stay focused, and let patience make you into the person God has always intended for you to be!

TWELVE
Unstoppable

"I know that you can do all things; no purpose of yours can be thwarted."— Job 42:2 (NIV)

- Satan, or your enemies, cannot stop the plans of God for your life! You may have had to wait; your blessings may have been held up; but God is bringing them forth now!

THIRTEEN
Amazing

"Look at the nations and watch—and be utterly amazed. For I am going to do something in your days that you would not believe, even if you were told."— Habakkuk 1:5 (NIV)

- God is amazing! He is about to blow your mind! Only believe!

FOURTEEN
Brilliant

"It shone with the glory of God, and its brilliance was like that of a very precious jewel, like a jasper, clear as crystal."— Revelation 21:11 (NIV)

- Girl, let your star shine! You light up a room when you enter it, and people are inspired by your charisma!

FIFTEEN

Funny

"And Sarah said, "God has made me laugh, and all who hear will laugh with me."— Genesis 21:6 (NKJV)

"A cheerful heart is good medicine, but a crushed spirit dries up the bones."— Proverbs 17:22 (NIV)

- Learn to laugh! Think of God's goodness toward you! You are about to experience a joy that is unspeakable and full of His glory!

SIXTEEN

A Great Mother

"As a mother comforts her child, so will I comfort you; and you will be comforted over Jerusalem."—Isaiah 66:13 (NIV)

- You are an awesome mother! Your children are going to rise and call you blessed! Your children will make you proud!

SEVENTEEN
A Great Daughter

"The father of a righteous child has great joy; a man who fathers a wise son rejoices in him."—
Proverbs 23:24 (NIV)

- Not only do your parents rejoice because you are a joy, but your father in heaven has great joy because of you! He truly adores you daughter!

EIGHTEEN
A Great Friend

"I no longer call you servants, because a servant does not know his master's business. Instead, I have called you friends, for everything that I learned from my Father I have made known to you."— John 15:15 (NKJV)

- People trust you with their secrets! God trusts you too! He wants to be your friend and is longing to spend time with you!

Des Taylor

NINETEEN

A Great Advice Giver

"A person finds joy in giving an apt reply; and how good is a timely word!"— Proverbs 15:23 (NIV)

"Like apples of gold in settings of silver Is a word spoken in right circumstances." — Proverbs 25:11 (NASB)

- You know what to say and when to say it! Don't be afraid to speak what God has been tugging on your heart to say!

TWENTY
Motivated & Energetic

"But I have prayed for you, Simon, that your faith may not fail. And when you have turned back, strengthen your brothers."— Luke 22:32 (NIV)

"For I am persuaded, that neither death, nor life, nor angels, nor principalities, nor powers, nor things present, nor things to come, nor height, nor depth, nor any other creature, shall be able to separate us from the love of God, which is in Christ Jesus our Lord."— Romans 8:38-39 (KJV)

- You are persuasive in your speech and attitude! Don't let anyone persuade you to turn away from your goals, dreams or visions! God will make them happen. Just stay focused!

TWENTY ONE
Inspirational

"For the LORD taketh pleasure in his people: he will beautify the meek with salvation."— Psalm 149:4 (KJV)

"The Lord GOD hath given me the tongue of the learned, that I should know how to speak a word in season to him that is weary: he wakeneth morning by morning, he wakeneth mine ear to hear as the learned."— Isaiah 50:4 (KJV)

- You do have the right words that can inspire or encourage someone – changing that person's life forever!

TWENTY TWO

Independent

"Abide in me, and I in you. As the branch cannot bear fruit of itself, except it abide in the vine; no more can ye, except ye abide in me."— John 15:4 (KJV)

- A part from God, you can do nothing! Abide in Him and he will give you success on every level!

TWENTY THREE
A Genius

"For who hath known the mind of the Lord, that he may instruct him? But we have the mind of Christ."— 1 Corinthians 2:16 (KJV)

"Let this mind be in you, which was also in Christ Jesus"— Philippians 2:5 (KJV)

- Thinking like Christ allows you to act/behave like He would! You are a genius, and he has given you creative power and ingenious ideas to change the world!

TWENTY FOUR
Determined

"Brethren, I count not myself to have apprehended: but this one thing I do, forgetting those things which are behind, and reaching forth unto those things which are before; I press toward the mark for the prize of the high calling of God in Christ Jesus."— Philippians 3:13-14 (KJV)

"Let us not lose heart in doing good, for in due time we will reap if we do not grow weary."— Galatians 6:9 (NASB)

- Don't ever, ever give up! It may get hard sometimes, but trust that God will give you the strength to bring you to your ultimate goal! You will make it to the other side!

TWENTY FIVE

Wise, Smart & Forward Thinking

"If any of you lacks wisdom, you should ask God, who gives generously to all without finding fault, and it will be given to you."— James 1:5 (NIV)

"I will do what you have asked. I will give you a wise and discerning heart, so that there will never have been anyone like you, nor will there ever be."— 1 Kings 3:12 (NIV)

- God has given you the understanding to make wise choices! Spend time in his presence and wait for Him to give you the right answers!

TWENTY SIX
Educated & Innovative

"But remember the LORD your God, for it is he who gives you the ability to produce wealth, and so confirms his covenant, which he swore to your ancestors, as it is today."— Deuteronomy 8:18 (NIV)

"As for these four children, God gave them knowledge and skill in all learning and wisdom: and Daniel had understanding in all visions and dreams."— Daniel 1:17 (KJV)

- God is the one who has given you the knowledge, understanding, and education you need to be successful! You can, and will, make a difference! Trust in your God-given abilities!

I Am

TWENTY SEVEN
A Great Homemaker

"A wife of noble character who can find? She is worth far more than rubies. Her husband has full confidence in her and lacks nothing of value. She sets about her work vigorously; her arms are strong for her tasks. She speaks with wisdom, and faithful instruction is on her tongue. She watches over the affairs of her household and does not eat the bread of idleness."— Proverbs 31:10-11;17;26-27 (NIV)

- You are a great wife and mother! Your instruction, wisdom, and quiet strength, are helping to build a lasting legacy!

TWENTY EIGHT

Goal Oriented & A High Achiever

"And we all, who with unveiled faces contemplate the Lord's glory, are being transformed into his image with ever-increasing glory, which comes from the Lord, who is the Spirit."— 2 Corinthians 3:18 (NIV)

- God is increasing you! You will be great and make an impact in society!

TWENTY NINE
Beautiful

"He has made everything beautiful in its time. He has also set eternity in the human heart; yet no one can fathom what God has done from beginning to end."— Ecclesiastes 3:11 (NIV)

"and provide for those who grieve in Zion-- to bestow on them a crown of beauty instead of ashes, the oil of joy instead of mourning, and a garment of praise instead of a spirit of despair. They will be called oaks of righteousness, a planting of the LORD for the display of his splendor."— Isaiah 61:3 (NIV)

- You are beautiful! You are exactly the way God wanted you to be! Stop comparing yourself to others' beauty standards! In God, there are no flaws! There is no one quite like you, so embrace it!

THIRTY

A Heroine

"And by a prophet the LORD brought Israel out of Egypt, and by a prophet was he preserved."—
Hosea 12:13 (KJV)

- God is sending you to be someone's hero! Be open to divine connections and appointments!

THIRTY ONE

Stable

"The Lord will establish you as his holy people, as he promised you on oath, if you keep the commandments of the Lord your God and walk in obedience to him."— Deuteronomy 28:9 (NIV)

"But the Lord is faithful, who shall establish you, and keep you from evil."— 2 Thessalonians 3:3 (KJ2000)

- Don't be afraid! Take courage in knowing that God's got you! Situations and people may change, but God will stabilize you!

THIRTY TWO

Entertaining

"The Lord is my strength and my shield; my heart trusted in him, and I am helped; therefore, my heart greatly rejoiceth; and with my song will I praise him."— *Psalm 28:7 (KJV)*

- Be happy and strong in the Lord! You bring so much joy to peoples' lives, and your jokes and laughter make someone's day!

THIRTY THREE

Strong, Courageous & Bold

"Have not I commanded thee? Be strong and of a good courage; be not afraid, neither be thou dismayed: for the LORD thy God is with thee whithersoever thou goest."— Joshua 1:9 (KJV)

- Don't be afraid! Accomplish your dream, leave that bad situation, or go back to school! Whatever your heart's desire, you can do it!

Know that God is with you every step of the way!

THIRTY FOUR

An Overcomer

"Yet in all things, we are more than conquerors and gain an overwhelming victory through Him who loved us [so much that he died for us]."— Romans 8:37 (AMP)

"And they overcame him by the blood of the Lamb (Jesus), and by the word of their testimony;"— Revelation 12:11 (KJV)

- You will get through this! Don't be discouraged, and don't give up! Keep pressing on until you see the finish line!

THIRTY FIVE
Adventurous

"And without faith it is impossible to please God, because anyone who comes to him must believe that he exists and that he rewards those who earnestly seek him."— Hebrews 11:6 (NIV)

"Thus also, faith by itself, if it does not have works, is dead."— James 2:17 (NKJV)

You are adventurous —not afraid to take risks or try something new! Keep walking by faith, and stepping out on God's word, and watch Him move for you!

THIRTY SIX
A Leader

"I have given you authority to trample on snakes and scorpions and to overcome all the power of the enemy; nothing will harm you."— Luke 10:19 (NIV)

"And hath made us kings and priests unto God and his Father; to him be glory and dominion for ever and ever. Amen."— Revelation 1:6 (KJV)

- You are a leader who can influence many! Take the authority that God has given you through Jesus' death on the cross! Fear not and take possession of what belongs to you!

I Am

THIRTY SEVEN
Healed

"But I will restore you to health and heal your wounds,' declares the LORD, 'because you are called an outcast, Zion for whom no one cares."— Jeremiah 30:17 (NIV)

"But he was wounded for our transgressions, he was bruised for our iniquities: the chastisement of our peace was upon him; and with his stripes we are healed." — Isaiah 53:5 (KJV)

- God has fully restored you back to how you

were before sickness entered your body! Decree and declare that your mind, soul, and body are healed in the name of Jesus Christ! You are whole, happy, and healthy!

THIRTY EIGHT
Powerful

"Finally, be strong in the Lord and in his mighty power."— Ephesians 6:10 (NIV)

"But you will receive power when the Holy Spirit comes on you; and you will be my witnesses in Jerusalem, and in all Judea and Samaria, and to the ends of the earth."— Acts 1:8 (NIV)

- In God and through God, you have the power to live right and to make things happen in your life that may seem impossible! You are powerful, and the only one to determine your destiny!

THIRTY NINE
Happy & Healthy

"A happy heart makes the face cheerful, but heartache crushes the spirit."— Proverbs 15:13 (NIV)

"Dear friend, I pray that you may enjoy good health and that all may go well with you, even as your soul is getting along well."— 3 John 1:2 (NIV)

- Decree and declare that you are happy and fulfilled, and that your physical, emotional and spiritual health, are intact!!

FORTY

Prosperous & Wealthy

"The wise have wealth and luxury, but fools spend whatever they get." — Proverbs 21:20 (NLT)

"May the LORD, the God of your ancestors, increase you a thousand times and bless you as he has promised!" — Deuteronomy 1:11 (NIV)

"For I will turn toward you [with favor and regard] and make you fruitful and multiply you,

and I will establish and confirm My covenant with you."— Leviticus 26:9 (AMP)

- If you are a giver, expect God to increase and multiply you in every area of your life!! You have enough to pay all of your bills and take care of your family! It's in Christ Jesus that all wealth (spiritual and natural) and blessings flow!

FORTY ONE
Resilient

"Be on your guard; stand firm in the faith; be courageous; be strong."— 1 Corinthians 16:13 (NIV)

"but the one who stands firm to the end will be saved."— Matthew 24:13 (NIV)

"With your help I can advance against a troop; with my God I can scale a wall."— Psalm 18:29 (NIV)

- When you get knocked down, get back up

again! It's not over until you no longer have breath in your body! God, who is full of compassion and love, gives us multiple chances!

- His grace is sufficient for you!
- Keep on pressing until you see the reward!

FORTY TWO
A Masterpiece & One-of-a-Kind

"Before I formed you in the womb I knew you [and approved of you as My chosen instrument], And before you were born I consecrated you [to Myself as My own]; I have appointed you as a prophet to the nations." — Jeremiah 1:5 (AMP)

- Know that there is no one like you! Embrace your flaws and your favorite attributes, because you are truly God's masterpiece and one-of-a-kind!

FORTY THREE

Worthy Of Love, Honor & Respect

"just as He chose us in Him before the foundation of the world, that we should be holy and without blame before Him in love, having predestined us to adoption as sons by Jesus Christ to Himself, according to the good pleasure of His will, to the praise of the glory of His grace, by which He made us accepted in the Beloved."— Ephesians 1:4-6 (NKJV)

"We love because he first loved us." — 1 John

4:19 (NIV)

- Because God loves you with a special kind of love, do not allow anyone to treat you with disrespect or contempt. Don't allow anyone to abuse you in any way! You are worthy of respect, worthy of love, and worthy of all the best things in life that God desires to give you!

FORTY FOUR

Plan Of Salvation

Do you know Jesus? I'd like for you to get to know him as your Lord and personal Savior today. The Bible says that Jesus is "the way, the truth, and the life," and no one can come to the Father except through Him [John 14:6]. Jesus is the only one who can help you with your self-esteem and identity issues, and help you navigate life's many curve balls! He loves you, and He has a great plan for your life [Jer. 29:11]! Keep reading to learn more!

1. Have faith. Believe that God is the ONLY, true and living God [Isa 44:6; Isa 43:10; Heb 11:1,6; Deut 6:4; Rom 10:17; John 20:29] and that He sent His only son to die for your sins so that you may have eternal life [John 3:16; John 10:30, Rev 1:8, Rom 1:3, John 1:1-14; Luke 22:69-70, Matt 1:21].

2. Repent of your sins. We are all sinners, meaning that we have all transgressed against the law or commandments of God [1 John 3-4; Rom 3:23-24]. The Bible lets us know that we were all 'born in sin and formed in iniquity (Psalm 50:1),' and the wages of sin result in death [Romans 6:23, Rev 20:14]. Therefore, God had to send someone to pay the penalty for us (read Gen. 3), so that we may have a chance of eternal life. Repentance is to "express sincere regret and remorse." Acknowledge yourself as a sinner, and turn away from wrong doing and/or behav-

I Am

ior that displeases God. Ask God to forgive you and to reign in your heart – to lead and guide all of your ways [Prov. 3:5-6].

3. Be baptized in the name of Jesus Christ for the remission of your sins. It was Jesus who came to earth to die for our sins [Heb 9:22, Heb 10:5, Heb 12:2, Isa 43:11, John 1:26, 29, 33; Acts 4:12, Acts 19:5]. Therefore, baptism [immersion in water] is an "outward expression of an inward cleansing" and demonstrates your being buried with Christ [sins washed away] and resurrecting as a new creation in Him [Col 2:12, Col 3:17; Acts 2:36-41; Rom 6:8-9].

4. Receive His Holy Spirit. God promised his disciples that he would not leave them without a comforter [John 14:18, 16]. The Holy Ghost is the birth of the spirit [John 3:5, Matt 3:11] and dwells within us. Holy Spirit was purchased by

the blood of Jesus [death on the cross], promised by Him to his disciples [John 14:26, John 15:26; John 19:30], and first outpoured on the day of Pentecost [Acts 2:4; Joel 2: 28-29; Acts 2:15-18]. God promises that after we receive this precious gift [through the evidence of speaking with other tongues as the spirit of God gives the utterance (i.e., heavenly language), we will have power [Acts 1:8]! The Holy Spirit also refreshes us and gives us rest [Isaiah 28: 11, 12].

5. Live a holy, righteous life. Salvation is deliverance from all sin and unrighteousness. Of course we can only live holy/godly through Christ's help [Acts 2:36-41; Romans 8:5-9, 37]. The blood of Jesus cleanses us from all sin and sanctifies us (sets us apart/regenerates us) through God's grace [1 John 1:7; Rom 6:14; Eph 2:8]. It is through Jesus Christ that we 'have life, and have it more abundantly' [John

10:10; Eph 3:20; Matt 6:33]!

Welcome into the Kingdom! Be sure to build your relationship with God through prayer and reading/studying His holy scriptures every day [Psalms 1; Joshua 1:8-9, Prov. 3:32; Psalm 119:11; Acts 17:11; Rom 14:17; Luke 24:45; 2 Tim 3:16].

Remember: You are not alone. Jesus loves you! His Spirit will lead and guide you into all truth [John 14:26-27; John 15:1, 5; John 16:13], and help you to live a life that pleases our Heavenly father!

About The Author

Des Taylor has a passion for people, with a desire to see them reach their fullest potential. Born in Seville, Spain, Des spent her formative years in the Kentucky Derby Region, and the Historic Selma, Alabama, the birthplace of the Civil Rights Movement. Des has worked as a journalist/reporter for the State of Alabama's oldest and historic newspaper *The Selma Times-Journal*, interviewing foot soldiers and leaders of the Civil Rights Movement as well as city, state and national public figures, dignitaries, and celebrities. Her favorite writings include that which allow her to tell the stories of the unsung heroes that inspire, empower, and impact others. Having professional experience in Public Relations and Marketing in Higher Education and for a nonprofit law firm in Alabama, she has also worked in television advertising for a Fox affiliate in Montgomery, AL.

With a Bachelor of Arts in Communications/Dramatic Arts from Auburn University-Montgomery, and a Master of Science in Strategic Communication from Troy University, Des is a lifetime member of Phi Kappa Phi Honor Society and Omicron Delta Kappa Leadership Honor Society. She has won awards from the Alabama Press Association; is published by United Press International (UPI) and Google News; and her work has also been featured in Jet Magazine and other print and online publications. Des enjoys reading/studying the Bible, traveling, surfing the Internet for Celebrity News, and spending time with her five sisters, nephews and nieces, in her spare time.

Reference

1. Franklin D. Roosevelt. First Inaugural Address. http://www.americanrhetoric.com/speeches/fdrfirstinaugural.html Accessed October 21, 2017.

Index

A

abilities, 15, 47, 89

authority, 12, 63, 89

B

blood, 59, 84, 89

C

celebrities, 86, 89

chastisement, 66, 89

children, 33, 47, 89

Christ, Jesus, 67, 78, 83, 85

commandments, 55, 82, 90

confident, 6, 15, 90

conquerors, 12, 59

courage, 55, 57, 90

courageous, 8, 15, 57, 74

covenant, 47, 73

D

death, 19, 38, 82, 84

deliverance, 84, 90

despair, 27, 52, 90

dignitaries, 86

dreams, 18, 22, 39, 47, 57, 90

E

earth, 68, 83, 90

enemies, 29, 63, 90

experience, 32, 90

F

faith, 38, 61, 74, 82, 91

forsaken, 27, 91

funny, 7, 16, 32, 91

G

glory, 31–32, 63, 78, 91

gold, 23, 37, 91

grace, 75, 78, 85, 91

guide, 83, 85, 91

H

health, 66, 70, 91

heart, 13, 37, 43, 45, 56–57, 70, 83, 91

Holy Spirit, 68, 83–84, 92

I

iniquities, 66, 82, 92

insecurities, 11

instruction, 50, 92

intelligence, 17, 92

J

joy, 13, 32, 34, 37, 52, 56, 92

K

Kingdom, 85, 92

knowledge, 17, 47

L

laugh, 32, 92

leader, 8, 63, 92

life, 13, 19, 28–29, 38, 68, 73, 79, 81, 85, 92

N

nations, 30, 76, 93

O

outcast, 66

P

patience, 28, 93

Patient, 6, 28, 93

person, 37, 93

power, 26, 38, 63, 68, 84, 93

praise, 16, 52, 56, 78, 93

principalities, 38, 93

prize, 22, 43, 93

prophet, 54, 76, 93

R

refreshes, 19, 84

relationship, 85, 94

Resilient, 8, 74, 94

righteous life, 84

S

salvation, 8, 40, 81, 84, 94

seasons, 17, 40, 94

self-esteem, 81

servants, 35, 94

sickness, 12, 67, 94

sins, 82–84, 94

skills, 21, 47, 94

strength, 44, 56, 94

T

tongues, 40, 50, 84, 95

trust, 35, 44, 48, 95

truth, 81, 85, 95

U

unrighteousness, 84

V

victory, 59, 95

visions, 20, 39, 47, 95

W

watches, 30, 50, 61, 95

wealth, 47, 72–73, 95

weary, 40, 43

wisdom, 17, 45, 47, 50, 95

www.ingramcontent.com/pod-product-compliance
Lightning Source LLC
Chambersburg PA
CBHW071533080526
44588CB00011B/1658